THE COACHING REVOLUTION

An Interactive Guide to Finding Joy and Excellence in Coaching

Written by Seth Taylor
and Patrick Ianni

An Ianni Training Product

adidas
XBOX
SOUNDERS FC
MLS

A Note From A Fellow Coach

The experience you're about to have is about a cultural revolution in youth sports. It is going to create a richer experience of coaching for you and help you find ways to connect with your players on a deeper and more meaningful level while also boosting their best performance.

After a 30 year journey through youth, college, and professional soccer, I learned that we are not defined by how many championships we've won, but by the quality of our relationships. I learned this because after everything I accomplished in my career, I found I still lacked a sense of identity; a knowledge of who I was, on and off the field. Through some very transformative therapeutic experiences like the ones in this guidebook, I came to the realization that I had been trying to find my identity through playing soccer. All of the things I carried inside of me seemed to show up in everything I did, whether I wanted them there or not. It was this awareness that began to create a shift in me.

I've now gained the awareness that what we are doing everyday in coaching is creating our future. If we as coaches become aware of what we carry within us, we can heal the hurt and pass on the goodness. Change and love will become our legacy. And our players will be able to find what they are truly capable of. And we will find more joy on the sideline.

Welcome to the Revolution.

Patrick Ianni
Founder, Ianni Training
US Olympian, 2x MLS Cup Champion

Not I, nor anyone else can
travel that road for you.

You must travel it by yourself.
It is not far. It is within reach.

Perhaps you have been on it
since you were born, and did
not know.

Perhaps it is everywhere - on
water and land.

Walt Whitman, ***Leaves of Grass***

Introduction

Being A Coach

Whether you have chosen coaching as your profession, are temporarily coaching for this chapter in your life, or are coaching because it is a natural movement out of your competitive playing days, there is a truth that must sooner or later be acknowledged about this vocation: Coaching is deep... way deep. If we choose to view coaching as the same as working in retail or business or some other industry, we are doing a huge disservice to ourselves and the families we are serving. Coach is a position of profound importance in a child's life. Most of us can recall, without much effort, some significant impact a coach made in our lives, for better or worse. They were somehow key in our development and played a different role from Mom or Dad. Coaches were a testing ground for many of us. For some of us, they supplemented our home life with the care and love they showed. Some of us were hurt by coaches. But anyone who has ever played youth sports was affected in some way or another by this prominent figure. The importance of our Coaches in our lives is why this book exists.

This Guidebook is a tool to educate and equip you for the task of raising your awareness of the deep issues in this profession and how they are affecting your coaching experience. If taken seriously and walked through mindfully, this Guidebook experience can give you a depth of understanding and a language with which to approach this unique element of your job. It will be deeper than you might expect and has the potential to transform your day-to-day life, on and off the field.

In addition to this Coach's Guidebook, we've created a complimentary Parent Guidebook called *On Frame: Exploring the Depths of Parenting in the World of Youth Soccer.* *On Frame* is specifically tailored to the unique emotional challenges of being a soccer parent. The hope is that parents will invest in this experience also, but remember, you're the leader in the relationship with the parents. If you use this experience to nurture in them a mutual understanding and language, it will save you time and energy as together, you navigate the development of these kids you've all been charged with caring for. Ultimately, this is about the kids; their development as players and people. But we were once those kids - and perhaps still are in some ways - so this is also very much about us.

How to Use This Guidebook

This Guidebook is a collection of teaching, guided journaling, and action-driven exercises. All the language and some of the teachings and activities will be similar or the same as what is contained within the Parents Guidebook. This is intentional so that new levels of helpful dialogue can emerge between you, the parents, and the players. Each of these activities is designed to bring your reflection inward to your experience of the nuances in relationships we encounter in the club soccer world. This experience is for you and designed completely with the goal of helping you experience as much joy and fulfillment as possible while skillfully developing your players, so a mindful approach will bring you - and your players - the most benefit. Simply move through the book in order and follow the easy-to-understand instructions over the next few weeks.

Before we begin, let's define some terms that will be helpful for you to understand as you go through the Guidebook. These terms will give you a helpful language in describing and understanding your coaching experience.

Awareness
(What is Conscious vs. What is Unconscious)

One of the main goals of this Guidebook is to raise your level of awareness. We use that term to mean simply this: you become deeply aware of how the unconscious world is affecting the conscious world at any given moment and in any given person, including and most importantly, within yourself. Most of what dictates our lives stems from our unconscious world, what we are not aware of, in some way. We tend to orient our relationships because of how we carry our life story deep within us: all the good and all the ugly parts of it. We tend to work from that place, love from that place, parent from that place, and coach from that place. And unfortunately, it is almost always the suffering that we experience in our lives that(subconsciously) drives our behavior, even if we don't realize it. Those who start to become aware of that fact are more empowered to make choices each day to change and improve their lives and relationships without having to suffer as much. These are the individuals who get better at what they do and at the same time become happier people. Therefore, the goal of experiences like those contained in this Guidebook is to help you accomplish a higher level of awareness. Yes, this will mean that deep things will be approached and reflected upon and, for it to be effective, it will require honesty and even vulnerability. But again, this experience is for you and you alone.

Trigger

Trigger is an often-used word in therapeutic circles and can have various meanings, but when it is used here, it will be referring to the moments we experience a severe rise in emotion (or an emotional shut down) and the things that cause that rise. These emotional experiences are often disproportional to the situation presenting itself. A good example might be something like this:

> **You have an ideal of the kind of coach you want to be, but when the whistle blows to start a match, you tend to become absorbed to the point where winning and losing clearly takes center stage. You get furious with refs and short with your players. You don't want to be that way, but it just seems to be the "way you are". In practice, you aren't that way, and you don't know what causes "the switch to flip."**

IIn this example, something about engaging in the competition of an actual game triggers you. Perhaps your mentality in practice is different, but something about games and the pressure they induce triggers unconscious energies and emotions in your body that you usually don't notice are there. These triggers are the key to unlocking our unconscious world. Each time the game or a player or parent triggers you, as difficult as that experience can be, you are being given a gift. You are being shown how your story and the things you carry within you intersect with the world around you. These parts of our story are often painful and are characterized by emotions like deep sadness and intense anger or even intense worry or depression. And this isn't reserved for only those of us who come from difficult backgrounds: it is the human condition.

If we are open to acknowledging how past life events and triggers affect our behavior today, we can start to experience our world with more compassion and less judgement - and that frees us to let people be who they are so that we can be the people we want to be. The great psychologist Carl Jung said: "We may think that we fully control ourselves. However, a friend can easily reveal something about us that we have absolutely no idea about." Now read that last sentence and replace the word "friend" with something like "referee" and you'll start to understand. This book will help you learn how to see what is being revealed to you by these triggers. And, as you may already know, the world of competitive sports is full of triggers for parents, kids, and coaches.

Speaking of Referees: A Note on the Fairly Obvious

Referees are a necessity in our game and it is fair to say that they tend to be triggers for most coaches. A large part of that is obviously because they have such a profound impact on the outcome of a game and thus the emotions of our players and their parents, not to mention our jobs. If we invest in the experience of this guidebook, our awareness will rise to a level that will allow us to take a deep breath before lashing out verbally at these men and women (and boys and girls) who take the time out of their lives to officiate our games. Yes, sometimes referees are not as good at their jobs as we would hope. But if our goal here is to produce healthy and successful athletes who live their life with courage and curiosity, then we can afford to let that poor call go and become aware of our inner experience. Our players and parents (as well as our own families) will thank us for it down the road. And, if we do this challenging internal work, we will become the model for how to handle with grace the many things in life that are out of our control.

Section 1

Your Players

Athletes need to enjoy their training. They don't enjoy going down to the track with a coach making them do repetitions until they're exhausted. From enjoyment comes the will to win.
Arthur Lydiard

A life is not important except in the impact it has on other lives.
Jackie Robinson

A coach is someone who can give correction without causing resentment.
John Wooden

The most profound task of the human race is the search for identity - a sense of Who We Are. The great psychologist Abraham Maslow called this "Self-Actualization" and placed it at the top of his famous "Hierarchy of Needs." Meaning, after we are able to take care of the basic needs of a human person, from things like air and food and water all the way up to love and connection, we can then turn our attention to our greatest human need - a healthy sense of Self. The way we develop this sense as children is essentially by unconsciously asking these two primary questions since birth: "What makes me safe?" and, "What makes me valuable?"

From the moment of our conception, we sought the answer to these questions from the source: Mom and Dad. The idea is that the unconditional love we received from that ultimate source would answer those questions in such a way that we could then move out into the world and ask other questions like: What can I do? What can I become? These questions would be answered by a world where we would take risks, create things, and generally see what we could accomplish. We would then be able to go back to the source of unconditional love to reconnect to our identity - our sense of safety and value and self - and then return once again to experiment with this thing called life. And this cycle would continue until our sense of self was so rooted deep inside that we would no longer require Mom and Dad to be the source, because the source would be within us. In a perfect world, this is how all of us would have grown up.

Unfortunately, we as humans struggle to love unconditionally. No matter how much Mom and Dad love us, the task of loving unconditionally is difficult. Therefore, for most of us, at a very young age (ages 0-10 are the primary developmental years) and still heavily engaged in the primary unconscious task of asking "What makes me safe?" and "What makes me valuable?", we began to look to other things to supplement our identity development as we grew. ***Enter youth sports.***

Youth Soccer Coaches experience just about every angle of this most profound issue. Perhaps they don't yet notice it, but every day they see children that are striving to find the answers to those two questions: "What makes me safe?" and "What makes me valuable?" They see the confusion that kids experience in trying to earn something that wasn't meant to be earned (namely, love and security). They see the stress and frustration it causes. And they spend far too much energy dealing with parents that are seemingly unaware of that problem. Most coaches themselves are likely unaware of this problem because they deal with these same questions regarding identity deep within themselves; most adults do at some level.

Our claim is that who you are has a profound impact on what you do, but these things are not the same thing. Therefore, in this first section, we're going to spend some time reflecting on the concept of identity. And in that experience, we will lay the foundation for a greater understanding of the players and parents we deal with in our vocation every day.

"Your visions will become clear only when you can look into your own heart. Who looks outside, dreams; who looks inside, awakes."
Carl Jung

Exercise 1
Remember When

This first exercise will be much like writing and reading an old diary entry. In the boxes below, you will write your top 5 most memorable moments connected to your sporting universe as a child. The only guideline is that the memory be an interaction with an adult (as opposed to winning a trophy or something like that). An example may be something like a confrontation with a coach in practice, or a moment that your father told you he was proud of you, or perhaps a time you felt shamed for making a mistake. Start by just writing down your memories and once you have five of them, spend some time ranking them according to their level of impact on you.

As we raise our awareness of what our identity is made of, and therefore what our players are really experiencing, we must remember who we are and where we came from. Some of these memories may be full of joy and life and some of them may be painful.

Whichever they are, breathe deeply and try to remember why they hold that Top 5 spot. In the space below each box, rate by percentage whether that memory had a positive or negative impact on you. It may be both equally (50% positive / 50% negative) or more positive than negative (70% positive / 30% negative), or vice-versa.

Remember, the physical act of writing these intense memories out is crucial for the experience of raising your awareness.

(Helpful note: there is extra note pages at the back of this book if you need more space for writing.)

Memory #1

First time playing Soccer - SBFC
Wasn't to involved - I like to think
I was advanced at creating space!
Dad - Yoohoo's after games!
Lot of players on field - didn't touch
ball much

Positive/Negative 90/10

Memory #2

Playing for 1st competitive club.
Working with Coach Johnny Pummill
Lot of games - I remember odd
shaped fields - goals located in
strange areas. We were avrge overall.
Played up age groups - lost a lot

Positive/Negative 80/20

Memory #3

OPD - [illegible] [illegible] State / Regional
selections - felt very nervous and a
lot of pressure before. Staff was
all from certain area - felt like
they knew every player already but
me - wasn't selected in the end
U13 / U14

Positive/Negative 50/50

I thought I played pretty well

did not enjoy even Training

Memory #4

Fury 89 - Larry Gleson

- New club - players from different economic background - well established already - Knee injury (MCL)

Coach expected me to play in a tournament. Dad had confrontations w/ a parent that we all heard say something

Positive/Negative 30/70

only positive experience was college ~~exposure~~

Memory #5

Recruiting process w/ Paul Conway.

Genuine - felt wanted. Good connection

Positive/Negative 100/

However these memories affected you and are still affecting you, having written them down will be helpful moving into the next exercise where we begin to bring this goal of understanding our identity - who we are - and how our coaches and parents shaped us through the sports universe - to a whole new level.

Exercise 2
The Watcher

This second exercise will be an experiential progression from the first. This exercise can be understood as meditative in nature. Meaning: it will involve more feeling than thinking and will require you to be silent at times.

The goal is to become what we call "The Watcher." The next three events you have, whether that is a competitive game, training session, or tryout of any sort, you are going to add a new element of the way you watch your team. **You're going to add the element of internal observation to the event.**

What that means is that you will attempt to notice what comes up for you in your thoughts, emotions, and body sensations during the session, and to notice patterns that occur in your experience of yourself during these sessions. This can be a very effective tool for raising your awareness of what you may carry in your unconscious and even perhaps help you see how you may have attached some of those things to your vocation, and thus your players' performance.

Clearly, this might trigger you - which can be helpful moving forward. Have this book and a pen or pencil with you as you do this and fill in the notes sections provided after your session/game. An example might be something as simple as:

At least once a game, you get really mad at a ref. In this exercise, you will prepare yourself for that moment and when it comes, instead of lashing out, you will remain silent, take a deep breath, and feel what your body is experiencing. In this way, we will begin to understand that the problem isn't the ref - nor is the problem us - the problem, in fact, seems to be inside of us. Feel your internal body - locate in your body the sensations that you experience when this type of trigger presents itself. In this moment, there is no need to act; just observe what you feel.

Some guidelines to help you make this an effective experience:

1. Try not to judge your experience as good/bad or healthy/unhealthy. Just allow whatever you experience to be what it is. Judgement allows us to categorize ourselves and others in a way that is unhelpful because it lacks acceptance of what is the actual reality. If we can't see ourselves with honesty and compassion, we can't ever move forward. So, just write down your observations and notice if you feel the need to judge yourself or others.

2. Obviously, we cannot be silent when we coach, but try to notice when it is the emotional trigger (not you) that makes you speak, like in the example above. In those moments, try to be silent. This will allow for observation of the internal experience.

3. Be conscious of your breathing. Breathe deeply and slowly. Our internal experience of our own story as we coach is first and foremost a bodily experience. We feel these things in all kinds of physical sensations. That is because it is human nature to trap and carry repressed emotions and energies in our bodies in a variety of ways. When we breathe deeply, it helps us be still and infuses our bodies with energy and awareness. So, slow down and be mindful in the experience - it won't help you to rush through this.

4. Finally, no detail is too small to notice. This is an exercise to raise your awareness of you. So, leave nothing out. Scribble in the margins if you must. There is also extra journaling space in the back pages of this Guidebook, so feel free to write a page number on them and keep going if you need to. Again - for these three events, you are going to do things differently, with a different goal in mind. After them, feel free to return to whatever methods you see as best for you.

Location **Date** / /

Location **Date** / /

Location **Date** / /

Go back and read your journal entries. Have any patterns developed? What's the good? What do we want to change? How can we change those patterns?

Feeling that I didn't reach a certain level based on the potential I had - unwilling to get out of a comfort zone - take risks

It's not regret - try to use it as motivation as a coach to seek to improve myself and give my best for players

2 goals as a coach:

(1) Enjoy playing football (inspire love for the game)

(2) helped them improve / cared about them as an individual

Coaching not about passing on knowledge - its about creating a learning environment - experience problems - look for solutions - coach & players

As you did this exercise, what parts of yourself did you see that perhaps you hadn't noticed before? Or perhaps a better question to ask is: What did you discover was standing with you on that sideline as you coached? Did you see or feel any connection between how you approached performance in your childhood and what you project onto your players? Can you see how you might be subconsciously asking the people around you (especially your players) to carry some of your internal burdens?

Remember - these observations are best made without judgement. There is no right or wrong way to do this; there is simply what is. If we can approach it without judgement, we can ask more helpful questions regarding what we want from this coaching experience

"I never teach my pupils, I only attempt to provide the conditions in which they can learn.".

Albert Einstein

So, what is it you want from this coaching experience? That may seem like a straightforward question but, if you recall those two important questions you started asking when you were born - "What makes me safe?" and "What makes me valuable?" - then understand that you are likely still asking one or both of those questions, as most of us are. And in this culture, we all tend to look to our vocations to answer those questions for us, just as our players look to the game to give them that sense of identity.

This is why we must insist to our players that soccer not become a surrogate parent. We must coach them in a way that gives them the courage to try and fail and try and fail until success is a marker on their life path as opposed to a trophy that makes them feel safe and valuable.

Exercise 3
Being Known

This exercise is a simple one in getting to know your players a bit. You might know them pretty well already, but this can advance some of that knowledge and help to remind you that they are human beings asking complex internal questions all the time.

The format is simple: fill in the blanks after asking your players the questions listed. Feel free to come up with your own questions also – as long as you mix fun questions like, "What is your favorite food?" with "What is something that makes you angry?" A good way to begin is to ask one question per practice. Ask the question before the session and write them down as you go.

For instance, if you begin a practice by asking each player, at some point in the session, to come up to you and whisper in your ear one thing they are afraid of, the young ones will turn it into a game and the older ones will begin to think deeply. Some will surprise you and some will show you that they are afraid of that level of vulnerability.

Of course, don't make this "mandatory." But you will likely have a strong response that will give you a new understanding of the kids you are coaching and that is no small thing. For older kids, it might be much more difficult to be honest and remember that it isn't your job to fix their situations – you are there to listen and then become aware of who they are and what they need. And coaching from that place of awareness is a more empowering experience.

Questions:

1. What is your favorite thing we do in training?

2. Name one thing you are afraid of.

3. Describe what love is in one phrase

4. How does losing make you feel?

5. Name one place in the world you want to go and why.

This practice can be adopted as a regular thing. It allows you to show your players that they are safe in sharing their thoughts and feelings. It can establish a base of knowledge and comfort as well. If your team is going through a losing streak, you can start practice by asking every player to come to you at some point and give one reason that they think the team is struggling.

You can do the same for a winning streak. You might learn something you were missing and the communication lines will open up. Knowledge will grow as players observe that you care about what they think and feel.

Again, you don't have to resolve things for them, just listen. For most kids, taking some time to listen is enough for them to begin to trust you to teach them.

Player Name:

Player Name:

Player Name:

Player Name:

Player Name:

Player Name:

It is easier to build strong children than to repair broken men.

Frederick Douglass

Section 2

The Parents

Through the blur, I wondered if I was alone or if other parents felt the same way I did - that everything involving our children was painful in some way. The emotions, whether they were joy, sorrow, love or pride, were so deep and sharp that in the end they left you raw, exposed and yes, in pain. The human heart was not designed to beat outside the human body and yet, each child represented just that - a parent's heart bared, beating forever outside its chest.

Debra Ginsberg

That's the beauty of coaching. You get to touch lives, you get to make a difference. You get to do things for people who will never pay you back and they say you never have had a perfect day until you've done something for someone who will never pay you back.

Morgan Wootten

But kids don't stay with you if you do it right. It's the one job where, the better you are, the more surely you won't be needed in the long run.

Barbara Kingsolver

It's probably not a stretch to say that the biggest challenge that youth soccer coaches face is not on the playing field and it's not in the actual coaching and dealing with their players; it's in finding the right ways to communicate effectively with parents.

Many coaches spend tremendous amounts of energy dealing with political and social issues that are generated for one reason or another by parents of their players. They can be anything from minor questions over text and email to intense drama stemming from parents who are triggered and unaware, often unwilling to look into themselves as the possible source of the conflict. This is one of the main goals of the Guidebook experiences for coaches and parents: to save coaches as much of their energy as possible by eliminating a substantial amount of drama through an elevated awareness of the internal experience of these things.

The ultimate beneficiary of this awareness is, of course, the kids. The higher level of awareness that parents and coaches have of how they carry their own unconscious beliefs and experiences, the more kids will be free of having to "caretake" the emotions and needs of the adults. And thus, they will be free to have their life at home (where love is) separate from their life on the field (where they find out what they can do).

"Care-taking" is when a child becomes unconsciously aware that in order to gain the love they need to form a healthy identity, they must suppress or sacrifice a part of themselves to appease the source of that love.

They learn what is safe to feel and believe and what is not. In children, this dynamic mainly presents itself in their relationship with their parents; and many people grow up having gained a powerful unconscious drive to care-take those they are in closest relationship with. Many coaches care-take parents a great deal and thus sacrifice parts of themselves constantly in ways that lead to burnout and frustration.

In Exercise 1, we are going to have a look at what it means to avoid care-taking the parents of our players and we will do some examination of ourselves in order to find a healthier way of relating. The result of this rising awareness will be that we can speak the truth in relationship with people and then be empowered to become the best coaches we can be, independent of the drama that is all too common in youth sports culture.

Note: The exercises in this section were designed with the knowledge that some of the coaches going through this Guidebook have tremendous amounts of experience and even success in dealing with parents over the years and also that many coaches are parents themselves. But if walked through mindfully, even experienced coaches can gain some further insight into why parents do what they do. These insights can help them further develop their thinking and language in dealing with these issues. It can also help a great deal in articulating this wisdom and knowledge for younger, less experienced coaches to learn from.

Parents are the ultimate role models for children. Every word, movement and action has an effect. No other person or outside force has a greater influence on a child than the parent.

Bob Keeshan

Exercise 1
FAQs

Parent meetings are not unlike a performance for coaches. Coaches get on stage, try to make the right impression, and hope to lay down the foundation for good communication over the coming season. They also start to get a feel right away of who in the group of parents will likely require the most maintenance.

Throughout a season, many coaches have a system of communication that they use; policies in place that dictate how things will go in parent/coach relationships. Sometimes these policies are handed down from the club, but often they are just things that a coach works out through trial and error.

The following exercise is going to be about truth-telling. We're going to spend the next few pages laying out a framework for what we want to say to parents. Each page will have some guidance in the form of frequently asked questions from parents. If you take the time and focus on what you're experiencing as you write, this could be very helpful for you.

Go slow and breathe deeply. For each question asked of you by a parent, you will begin by writing the unfiltered answer. Spare NOTHING in your answer. Let every feeling you have out - be funny, sarcastic or harsh if you want. But above all, be HONEST. When you have gone through the 5 questions, you'll be given space to rewrite the answer in a way that is more realistic and less inflammatory. The goal is that you keep the truth, but lose the damaging parts.

When you're done, you should have something left to say that is honest, but not demeaning - and that kind of honesty diminishes drama. It will lessen the gossip among the parents and make the boundaries clear. And it will also reveal to you where you hold anger and frustration within your experience. That elevated awareness will be infinitely helpful moving forward as you deal with this sometimes-volatile social space.

The Passive Aggressive

"Hey Coach – I was just wondering what you think (player's name) could work on so that he could maybe crack that starting lineup?"

UNFILTERED

Success At All Costs

"Hey Coach, I'm not questioning your perspective here, but I wanted to let you know that (player's name) has always been a better striker than a center back. If you put him/her up front, I know she/he will start scoring like crazy."

UNFILTERED

The Over-Sophisticated Dad

"Hey Coach, I noticed you switched to a 4-3-3 at halftime. I'd love to hear your reasoning for that. Have you considered what you guys could do in a 4-5-1? That could get you guys more unified in the back and let (player's name) up top get some space to run in behind."

UNFILTERED

You're Playing Favorites

"Hey Coach – I'm not one of those kinds of parents, but I will say that at this age, it feels more appropriate for kids to get equal playing time and it's clear that you are favoring some players over others. Can you explain yourself please because we pay a lot of money to see our son/daughter play, not sit on a bench."

UNFILTERED

Commitment Issues

"Hey Coach, I hope it's okay with you that my son/daughter will be missing every other practice and a couple tournaments this summer because of basketball. She/he really loves the balance of playing more than one sport. Thanks for understanding."

UNFILTERED

Feels good to be that honest, right? Now, so that we don't start fires we can't put out, just go back and edit a bit. Take out direct insults and any profanity or sarcasm that may have been used. But, and I can't emphasize this enough, leave the honesty

The Passive Aggressive

"Hey Coach – I was just wondering what you think (player's name) could work on so that he could maybe crack that starting lineup?"

EDITED

Success At All Costs

"Hey Coach, I'm not questioning your perspective here, but I wanted to let you know that (player's name) has always been a better striker than a center back. If you put him/her up front, I know she/he will start scoring like crazy."

EDITED

The Over-Sophisticated Dad

"Hey Coach, I noticed you switched to a 4-3-3 at halftime. I'd love to hear your reasoning for that. Have you considered what you guys could do in a 4-5-1? That could get you guys more unified in the back and let (player's name) up top get some space to run in behind."

EDITED

You're Playing Favorites

"Hey Coach – I'm not one of those kinds of parents, but I will say that at this age, it feels more appropriate for kids to get equal playing time and it's clear that you are favoring some players over others. Can you explain yourself please because we pay a lot of money to see our son/daughter play, not sit on a bench."

EDITED

Commitment Issues

"Hey Coach, I hope it's okay with you that my son/daughter will be missing every other practice and a couple tournaments this summer because of basketball. She/he really loves the balance of playing more than one sport. Thanks for understanding."

EDITED

Exercise 2

Let It Role

The following exercise is a progression from the last and is also an exercise that is included in the "Your Coach" section of the Parent Guidebook. The goal of this exercise is to examine what our beliefs are regarding the different roles that coaches and parents play in helping a young athlete succeed. These roles are distinctively different and a lot of the problems encountered by children in youth sports stems from these roles encroaching upon one another.

The reason this happens usually dwells in the unconscious beliefs about these roles, shaped when we were kids. And that goes for coaches and parents alike. Many times, coaches unconsciously begin to step into the parents' role just like so many parents spend far too much energy coaching their children. We can't fix all of that in a few short weeks but if we can raise our awareness of these things, we will be empowered to approach these parts of ourselves with curiosity and courage, knowing that ultimately our children will benefit greatly from this.

The following grid shows various roles in a young athlete's life. Each of these roles is vital for them to reach their fullest potential. Under the text, there is a box with sections of writing space: one for parents (left), kids (center), and coaches (right). Write in each box which percentage of that particular role belongs to the parents, which belongs to the kid, and which to the coach. And then write a sentence or two explaining why you came to that conclusion. For example, a younger child may not be responsible for his/her own nutrition, but a 16-year-old might shoulder more, but not all, of that responsibility.

Also, be aware that every coach, just like every parent, has strengths and weaknesses, so there is a nuance in this exercise. If, for instance, you are a strong communicator with your players, then perhaps the parents won't need to support you in that area as much. That being said, learning to observe your own strengths and weaknesses without judgement, as well as those of your parents and players, can be very helpful.

Logistics

Making sure kids have all of the equipment necessary to train and perform well.

Parents ☐ % **Kids** ☐ % **Coach** ☐ %

Reasons why: ____________________

____

____

____

Nutrition

Making sure that kids take care of their bodies in regard to sleep, food, fitness, and hydration.

Parents ☐ % **Kids** ☐ % **Coach** ☐ %

Reasons why: ____________________

____

____

____

Identity Affirmation

Making sure your kids feel accepted, loved, seen, and heard no matter what they do or believe.

Parents ☐ % **Kids** ☐ % **Coach** ☐ %

Reasons why: ____________________

____

____

____

Critique/Coaching

Making sure that kids receive feedback as to the technical and tactical strengths and weaknesses of their game as well as what mentalities to adopt for training and games.

Parents ☐ % ***Kids*** ☐ % ***Coach*** ☐ %

Reasons why: ____________________

____

____

____

Opportunity

Making sure your kids have the right amount of game opportunity to test what they are learning in training and reap the rewards of the time they put in.

Parents ☐ % ***Kids*** ☐ % ***Coach*** ☐ %

Reasons why: ____________________

____

____

____

Performance Affirmation

Making sure kids feel that the work they put in doesn't go unnoticed and that those that know them are proud of what they accomplish.

Parents ☐ % ***Kids*** ☐ % ***Coach*** ☐ %

Reasons why: ____________________

____

____

____

At this point, you can probably see that there is a distinct difference between the role of a parent and the role of a coach in helping a child succeed. The tricky part is knowing where those lines are drawn and having the foresight, wisdom, and self-control to respect those lines.

It is our belief that the more honest and vulnerable we become in talking about these things with the parents on our team, the more this understanding will present itself as the dominant mentality

Success is never final, failure is never fatal. It is courage that counts.

John Wooden

It's important to remember that being a Parent cannot be fully understood unless you experiece it.

The complexity of emotion that parents feel for their children is almost beyond comprehensio.It's like an ice-berg: most of what's happening is under the surface, in the unconscious.

If you are a coach that has kids, you are probably nod-ding in agreement right now. If you don't have children, try to imagine your heart jumping out of your chest, strapping on cleats and shin guards, and then running around on a field, trying to see if it can survive.

That's what it feels like.

A coach that is aware of these things is much more prepared to fulfill his/her role to its full capacity and also deal with the moments of madness where complex emotions spill over.

The ultimate beneficiary of this deeper awareness and understanding are the players

Section 3

Yourself

It takes courage...to endure the sharp pains of self-discovery rather than choose to take the dull pain of unconsciousness that would last the rest of our lives.

Marianne Williamson

Man cannot discover new oceans unless he has the courage to lose sight of the shore.

Andre Gide

A life of frustration is inevitable for any coach whose main enjoyment is winning.

Chuck Noll

In the introduction to Section 1, we talked about how human beings form their identity by asking two very foundational questions: "What makes me safe?" and "What makes me valuable?"

We talked about how if those questions never really get answered in those developmental years between 0 and 10, then we keep asking them well into our adult lives. A large percentage of the struggles we face in life come to us because we are still searching for those answers. The people around us take on the unconscious task of communicating to us that we are safe (love) and valuable (vocation). What is really happening is that our relationships with people and our jobs are being asked to *re-parent* us - and they are simply not capable of doing that.

Competitive arenas like coaching soccer are filled with experiences that will cause us to fail *by design*. And if that failure, by our players and teams, is unconsciously experienced as a lack of love, (which it is by a lot of us) then doing a job like coaching can feel threatening and stressful.

Often times, our players catch the flack for our own unconscious struggles. The phenomenon known as *burnout* can be attributed to this type of dynamic. A coach is doing everything they can to be successful at their job, but for some reason, they can't find the fulfillment and joy they want to experience. Again, this is often because unconsciously, we're asking the job to *parent* us - to tell us we are safe and we are valuable - and it was never meant to do that.

Soccer is a game played on a field where players go and test themselves and ask themselves what they can create and become. It was never meant to love them or be anything other than a testing ground.

At its best, the joy that flows from the experience of the game is one where we see ourselves grow as we keep coming back to the testing ground. It is the place where we discover who we are.

But our identity is meant to be found within, in an unconditional love we develop for ourselves.

In this final section of the Guidebook, we are going to spend some time looking at who we are and who we want to become. The goal is to be able to walk away with a new paradigm of what "vocation" really is, with a freedom that can help us experience more joy and success on and off the field.

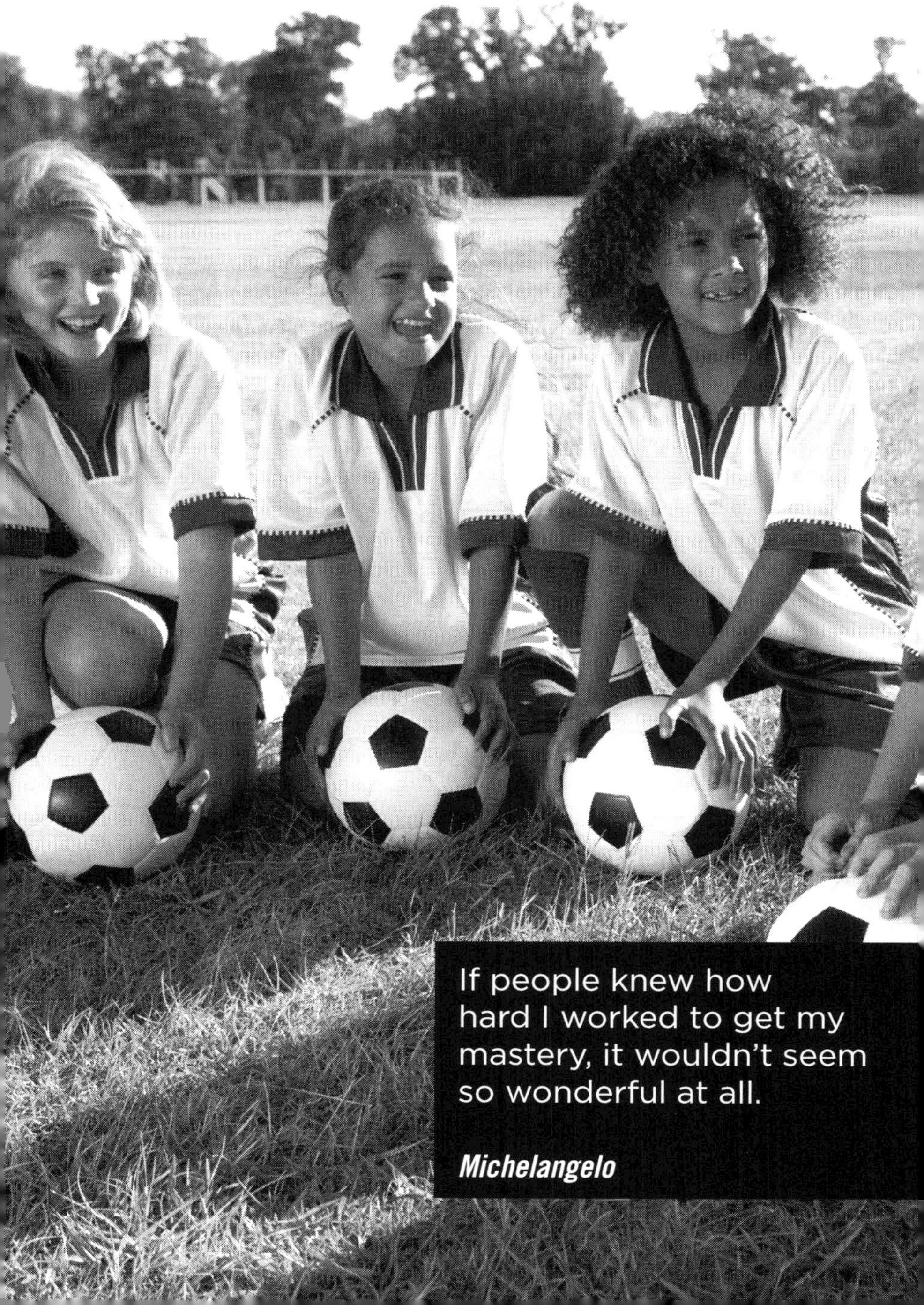

If people knew how hard I worked to get my mastery, it wouldn't seem so wonderful at all.

Michelangelo

Exercise 1

Why I Coach

This exercise is going to create a map for you to follow as you set goals for what kind of experience you want to have in your coaching as you move forward. And like the old saying goes, to know where you're going, you have to know where you've been.

So, we're going to do some introspection as to why you coach. ***Why did you start? Why do you continue to coach? And what is it that will keep you coaching?***

The format is pretty simple: Each box will have a space for you to the reasons why you coach. In between each box is a space to write about a life transition that may have changed the reasons you do things. An example might be that you had children or got married or moved to a new city sometime between when you started and now. These transitions may have changed you in a way that makes your reasons for coaching now different than your reasons for coaching when you started. There is also a section to write about transitions that you hope to make that may affect your reasons for coaching in the future. Under each box, you will see a scale of 1-10. This is to rate your enjoyment of coaching; 1 being the lowest level of enjoyment a person could have at a job and 10 being that you absolutely love coming to the field every day.

Remember, if you don't know why you coach, that is completely okay. Having a greater awareness of that will be helpful for you as you move forward as well. Take your time with these and give a real assessment as to what it is about this job you enjoy or don't enjoy.

Why did I start coaching?

Reasons:

Enjoyment Rating 1-10

Important Life Transitions

Why do I continue to coach?

Reasons:

Enjoyment Rating 1-10

Important Life Transitions

What will keep me coaching in the future?

Reasons:

Enjoyment Rating 1-10

Future Transition Goals

Exercise 2

Why I Coach

As a progression from the last exercise, let's do some analysis of our strengths and weaknesses as a coach.

The following chart has a list of important elements of coaching. Your job is to rate yourself on a scale of 1-10 in each category: 1 being "Needs major overhaul" and 10 being "Master."

In the final box, there are several ways to immediately improve that area, if you possess the courage to take action. If you find a weakness in your coaching in any area, circle one suggestion (or write one in yourself) that you will take to improve that area.

Remember that most of these suggestions will improve your life in more ways than just coaching.

Category: Tactical Understanding

Skill	(circle your rating)
Team Attacking	POOR • • • OK • • • MASTER
Team Defense	POOR • • • OK • • • MASTER
Set Pieces	POOR • • • OK • • • MASTER

Suggestions for Improvement *(Things I will try)*

- ☐ Find a mentor who is strong in this area of coaching.
- ☐ Study Film weekly with another Coach.
- ☐ Ask questions until they are answered.
- ☐ *Your Ideas* ____________________

Category: Technical Development

Skill	(circle your rating)
Training Session Design	POOR • • • OK • • • MASTER
Making the Game Fun	POOR • • • OK • • • MASTER
One-on-One Coaching	POOR • • • OK • • • MASTER

Suggestions for Improvement *(Things I will try)*

- ☐ Find a mentor who is strong in this area of coaching.
- ☐ Seek understanding of Child Development.
- ☐ Learn to see kids as kids (not small adults).
- ☐ *Your Ideas* ____________________

Category: Psychology

Skill	(circle your rating)
Personal Emotional Health	POOR • • • OK • • • MASTER
Player Health (Emotional/Psychological)	POOR • • • OK • • • MASTER
Competitive Psychology	POOR • • • OK • • • MASTER

Suggestions for Improvement *(Things I will try)*

- ☐ Find a mentor who experiences their life and job the way you wish to experience yours.
- ☐ See therapy *(it is incredibly helpful)*.
- ☐ Ask other coaches for book recommendations.
- ☐ *Your Ideas* ______________________

____

Category: Communication

Skill	(circle your rating)
With Players	POOR • • • OK • • • MASTER
With Parents	POOR • • • OK • • • MASTER
With Other Coaches	POOR • • • OK • • • MASTER

Suggestions for Improvement *(Things I will try)*

- ☐ Go through your Guidebook again.
- ☐ See Therapy *(It is incredibly helpful)*.
- ☐ Ask other coaches about what works for them.
- ☐ *Your Ideas* ______________________

____

The Limit

Understand that there is virtually no limit to the level of coach you can become. If you feel like you are limited, take note of that. When you woke up this morning, you had certain abilities that could each be improved by taking just one action step forward.

The key to seeing that improvement manifest is to detatch yourself from the outcome.

What that means is that we don't ask the vocation (like coaching) to parent us, whether at a conscious or unconscious level. We don't ask it to love us. We don't ask it to tell us who we are. We simply allow it to be a daily expression of our desire to see what we are capable of accomplishing. We learn to be here and now as opposed to in the future, even as we set goals regarding where we want to go with our lives and careers.

Of course, as we do this, things like paychecks and trophies happen. But they are simply a part of the experience - they don't define us. And as we take one step forward at a time, the undeniable improvement of our craft transforms the quality of what we do, which leads to greater and greater opportunities. It also allows us to enjoy what we are doing. A job freed from the burdens of all of our unconscious needs is then able to be what it's meant to be. And teaching kids about *The Beautiful Game* is an awesome thing to get to do every day.

The way forward for any coach is one step at a time, whether you are just beginning or looking at one more season before retirement. And that step is presenting itself to us right now if we know how to see it. You might need to have a conversation with a difficult parent that you've been avoiding. You might need to spend some real time reflecting on your long term and short-term goals so that you can lock down the next steps of your evolution as a coach and as a person. Maybe it's time to stop talking about learning a meditative practice and start doing it one breath at a time.

The next exercise will be a discussion and some thinking about how to have a real plan for right now so we can take steps every day toward our future goals.

Remember, teamwork begins by building trust. And the only way to do that is to overcome our need for invulnerability.
Patrick Lencioni

Exercise 3

Goal Sandwich

The following exercise has a sandwich-type feel to it. It is a practical and simple way of writing out goals that could actually help as opposed to simply saying, "This is what I want to accomplish" (and hoping it comes about).

The idea is this: In the first section, you are going to write 3 goals you have for your experience of this year of coaching. The reason we say that this is about *your experience* as opposed to setting a goal to win a State Championship or something is because there are about a million things that you have no control over that must go right to win a trophy. This is why making it a primary goal to win a trophy will likely be unhelpful in moving you forward in life.

Instead, make your goals something like, *"I want to have at least 95% of my energies available to me each training session."* These kinds of goals have clear and simple action steps attached to them, such as: "Sleep at least 8 hours a night" and "Move away from coffee as my primary source of energy." And clearly, if you were to accomplish the goal of having 95% of your energies available to you every training session, the quality of what you do would go up quickly and things like trophies become realistic parts of the landscape in front of you.

But again, the present moment is the key to success.

Below are some prompt questions. Each question will be followed by spots to answer the question regarding three goals you have for your coaching this year. These questions are simple, fill-in-the-blank questions that will show you just how easy it is to create tangible action steps towards the improvement of your craft and life.

Finally, you'll write down three goals for your coaching career in 5 years. Make these more like levels to aspire to. An example could be something like, "*I want to be coaching an A team*," or "*I want to be making (number) of dollars per year coaching soccer.*" Make sure to take the time to think about it and write down the Top 3 goals for your life in 5 years.

What are the most basic and immediately accessible steps towards that goal. List at least 2. Make these steps that could be taken (or begun) in the next week.

Goal #1

Goal #2

Goal #3

Name two people you know that could give you good advice or help you take these steps. Write their names down. Write why you believe they can be helpful. Then write down how and when you will contact them regarding this goal of yours.

Goal #1

Goal #2

Goal #3

Finally, remember this: goal setting is about putting your intentions for your life and career in motion. If someone tells you "no" or you run into a barrier of some sort, that is guidance, not and end. Keep moving forward, no matter what.

Goal #1

Goal #2

Goal #3

Goals 5 years from now:

1.

2.

3.

Setting goals is the first step in turning the invisible into the visible. It is in your moments of decision that your destiny is shaped.
Tony Robbins

Conclusion

I've learned that people will forget what you said, people will forget what you did, but people will never forget how you made them feel.
Maya Angelou

To be yourself in a world that is constantly trying to make you something else is the greatest accomplishment.
Ralph Waldo Emerson

You must be the change you wish to see in the world.
Mahatma Gandhi

The main goal of this Guidebook is that you would begin to see that coaching, just like all vocations, is an experience you are having.

If we have just begun coaching, this is about finding out what coaching can teach us about ourselves: what we love or don't love and what our strengths and weaknesses are. For those in mid-life, it is much more about discovering what it means to become a master at something - to "be all you can be." And for those coaches who have been in the game for a long time, that path is the one of the Sage: the wise old man/woman that has experience and wisdom to give the world. Coaches span the length of that spectrum. For every John Wooden (perhaps the wisest of the coaching sages we have known in America), there's a young coach coming out of college, wanting to see what they can accomplish.

The key then becomes for each of us to know exactly where we are so we can set measurable and attainable goals for where we want to be. And make no mistake, if you are in the evening of your life and you are not a Sage (giving your wisdom to the world), know that you are *meant* to be. Hopefully, this Guidebook can help you see what is keeping you from that sacred task.

Take a step back and look at the *Goal Sandwich* you just created. As you do, you will see that becoming the people and coaches we want to be is about taking one small step at a time and letting that be enough, understanding that the outcome (or future) will take care of itself. And if you encounter those all too common stories that we tell ourselves about how "you don't deserve this" or "you aren't good enough to do that," then have the courage to take another small step towards facing the things in your life that have created those stories.

Remember, coaching is deep - way deep - and if we are going to be the ones to step onto the field and fulfill that important role in a child's life, then we must have the courage to not allow coaching to become simply something we do for a paycheck or to be something we do so that we can prove to ourselves we're good enough. Coaching is too important for that. And it will teach us about our own lives - if we are open to it.

We shall not cease from exploration
And the end of all our exploring
Will be to arrive where we started
And know the place for the first time.

T.S. Eliot

Notes

Share your experice of ***The Coaching Revolution*** at IanniTraining.com.

Also available from Ianni Training, *On Frame*

On Frame is an interactive guidebook, taking parents of young athletes on a journey through their own experiences and perspectives regarding how they approach the balance between being a loving parent and encouraging their child to push through challenges and excel in their endeavors.

Examining healthy and unhealthy approaches to competition, ***On Frame*** helps parents find their best self and teaches them how to be their student athletes' biggest asset in their sporting life, changing the competitive landscape of Youth Sports in America at a time when it is needed most.

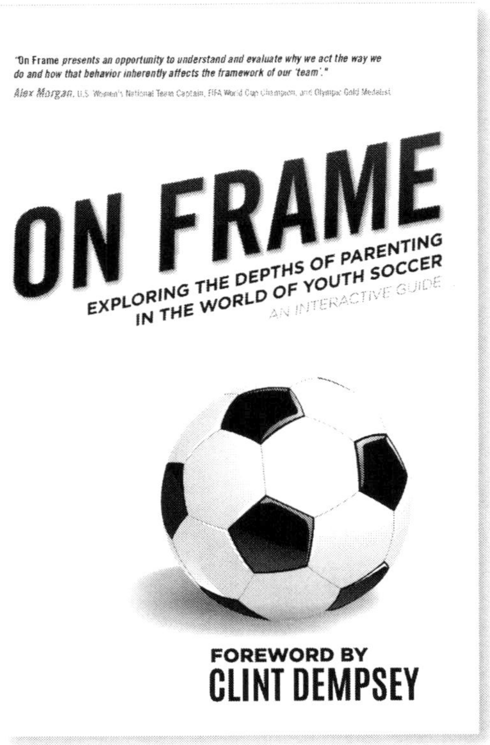

Let's get started! Find On Frame on Amazon.com!